THE CIVIL RIGHTS
MOVEMENT

Essential Events

THE CIVIL RIGHTS
MOVEMENT

BY JENNIFER JOLINE ANDERSON

Content Consultant
Keith Mayes, associate professor
University of Minnesota

ABDO
Publishing Company

CREDITS

Published by ABDO Publishing Company, 8000 West 78th Street, Edina, Minnesota 55439. Copyright © 2012 by Abdo Consulting Group, Inc. International copyrights reserved in all countries. No part of this book may be reproduced in any form without written permission from the publisher. The Essential Library™ is a trademark and logo of ABDO Publishing Company.

Printed in the United States of America,
North Mankato, Minnesota
062011
092011

♻ THIS BOOK CONTAINS AT LEAST 10% RECYCLED MATERIALS.

Editor: Paula Lewis
Copy Editor: Rebecca Rowell
Cover Design: Kazuko Collins
Interior Design and Production: Christa Schneider

Library of Congress Cataloging-in-Publication Data
Anderson, Jennifer Joline.
  The civil rights movement / by Jennifer Joline Anderson.
    p. cm. -- (Essential events)
  Includes bibliographical references and index.
  ISBN 978-1-61783-098-3
  1. African Americans--Civil rights--History--20th century--Juvenile literature. 2. Civil rights movements--United States--History--20th century--Juvenile literature. 3. United States--Race relations--Juvenile literature. I. Title.
  E185.61.A547 2011
  323.1196'073--dc22

                          2011010073

TABLE OF CONTENTS

Civil rights demonstrators at the Lincoln Memorial

"I Have a Dream"

On the morning of August 28, 1963, the atmosphere in Washington DC was tense. The streets were unusually empty for a Wednesday workday in the bustling capital. Police barricades had been erected, and President John F. Kennedy had put National Guard troops on alert in case of an outbreak of violence. A demonstration for civil rights was about to take place, and no one knew what to expect.

Buses and cars arrived by the hundreds and thousands. Airplanes and trains headed to the city. Crowds made their way to the Washington Monument. The 555-foot (169-m) obelisk was designated as the starting point for the March on Washington for Jobs and Freedom. The marchers were united in their demand of equality for African Americans. One hundred years after slavery had been outlawed in the United States, racial discrimination still prevented blacks from being treated as equal citizens.

What Are Civil Rights?

Civil rights are held by every adult citizen of a free nation. These rights include the right to vote, the right to a fair trial, equal protection under the law, freedom of speech, and freedom from discrimination on the basis of gender, race, religion, disability, age, or sexual orientation. The civil rights held by citizens of the United States are guaranteed in the Bill of Rights and other amendments to the US Constitution.

People spilled onto the monument grounds and carried signs demanding "JOBS for all NOW!" and "First-Class Citizenship NOW!" Many people wore their Sunday best. Some men wore fashionable, white porkpie hats. Others wore humble plaid shirts and denim to indicate they represented poor black

Leaders of the March on Washington, Martin Luther King Jr., left, and John Lewis, right, met with Senator Everett Dirksen, center, on August 28, 1963.

farmers from the South. The mood was joyful and optimistic as the masses began their slow march from the Washington Monument to the Lincoln Memorial, singing "We Shall Overcome."

Approximately 250,000 people marched for civil rights. Whites and blacks marched side by side. Religious leaders from the Catholic, Protestant, and Jewish faiths were present. Labor union organizers, politicians, and civil rights activists participated in the march.

In the Shadow of Lincoln

The crowd gathered before a stage that was erected on the steps of the Lincoln Memorial, which houses a marble statue of President Abraham Lincoln. Gathering at the site of the memorial was significant. It honored the man who, 100 years before, had signed the Emancipation Proclamation, freeing enslaved African Americans in the Confederate states. The program included speeches by civil rights leaders and music by famous performers.

John Lewis was among those who spoke. The 23-year-old was an activist in the civil rights movement and one of the leaders of the Student Nonviolent Coordinating Committee. In a fiery, controversial speech, Lewis accused Washington leaders of neglecting the issue of civil rights and said African

The Lincoln Memorial

The Lincoln Memorial was constructed from 1912 to 1922 to honor the sixteenth president of the United States, Abraham Lincoln. Built in the style of a classical Greek temple, it features a massive 19-foot (5.8-m) statue of a seated Lincoln carved from Georgia white marble. An image of the memorial appears on the reverse of the one-cent coin and the five-dollar bill.

Americans could wait no longer for real change. "If we do not get meaningful legislation out of this Congress," Lewis declared, "the time will come when we will not confine our marching to Washington." He continued his speech and added,

We will march through the South, through the streets of Jackson, through the streets of Danville, through the streets of Cambridge, through the streets of Birmingham. But we will march with the spirit of love and with the spirit of dignity that we have shown here today.[1]

The Civil Rights Act of 1964

The March on Washington expressed support for a law proposed by Kennedy in 1963. Kennedy proposed the bill because of the grassroots movement of blacks in Birmingham, Alabama. If the Civil Rights Act passed in Congress, it would make sweeping changes in the nation.

As a law, it would make discrimination on the basis of race, color, gender, religion, or nation of origin illegal. Businesses would not be allowed to discriminate. Segregation in public places such as libraries, schools, and restaurants would be illegal. Equal opportunities in schools and the workplace would be guaranteed. Some activists, including Lewis, felt the act was not strong enough to make a difference. Others hoped it would open the door to positive change.

The proposed law met with opposition in the legislature. But Senate Minority Leader Everett M. Dirksen stated, "It is essentially moral in character. It must be resolved. It will not go away. Its time has come."[2]

The president and civil rights supporters feared the act would not pass. Kennedy was assassinated in November 1963, but on July 2, 1964, after a year of deliberation and more protests, Congress passed the Civil Rights Act. President Lyndon Johnson then signed it into law.

A Man with a Dream

The last to speak that day was Reverend Martin Luther King Jr., a Baptist minister from Alabama who had emerged as one of the key figures of the civil rights movement. The 34-year-old King was a talented preacher. "Fivescore years ago," King began, "a great American, in whose symbolic shadow we stand today, signed the Emancipation Proclamation. . . . But one hundred years later, the Negro still is not free."[3] The time had come, King explained, to "cash a check" for the freedom owed African Americans; the time had come to "make justice a reality."[4]

In the final eight minutes of his speech, King spoke of a dream he held for America. Appealing to the values of freedom and equality on which the United States was founded, he said,

> *I have a dream that one day this nation will rise up and live out the true meaning of its creed: "We hold these truths to be self-evident: that all men are created equal." . . . I have a dream that my four little children will one day live in a nation where they will not be judged by the color of their skin but by the content of their character. . . . I have a dream today!*[5]

King's words were met with thunderous applause.

A Movement for All Americans

At the end of the day, the nation knew that the March on Washington had been a success. It had been the largest demonstration in US history, and there had been no angry mobs or bloodshed, only a great outpouring of public support for the cause of civil rights. As people all over the United States watched the event on television, many saw whites and blacks marching together in unity for the first time. This sent a powerful message: the civil rights movement was not only a movement for African Americans. It was a movement for all Americans. ⌐

*King gave his "I Have a Dream" speech during the
March on Washington on August, 28, 1963.*

In the early seventeenth century, slaves were brought to Virginia.

From Slavery
to Segregation

*I*n 1619, a Dutch ship bearing 20
Africans arrived at the English colony of
Jamestown, Virginia. These were the first Africans
to arrive in the British colonies of North America.
Over the following two centuries, more than half a

million Africans were brought into slavery in what is now the United States.

In 1784, Thomas Jefferson, who later became the nation's third president (1801–1809), proposed a ban on slavery in new territories after 1800. His proposal was narrowly defeated by the US Congress. In 1790, the first US census was taken. In a nation of approximately 3.9 million people, there were nearly 700,000 slaves—18 percent of the population. The Fugitive Slave Act of 1793 made it illegal for anyone to impede the capture of runaway slaves. A year later, with the invention of the cotton gin, the South had an increased need for slave labor.

By 1808, the importing of Africans for slave trade was made illegal, but slaves were smuggled in. The Missouri Compromise of 1820 settled the slavery issue for approximately 30 years. Missouri was admitted to the Union as a slave state and Maine as a free state. Slavery was then forbidden in new territories north of 36°30' north latitude, which was the southern boundary of Missouri. This solved the immediate issue and slavery in future states; however, it did not resolve the slavery issue.

Most slaves worked on tobacco, indigo, and cotton plantations in the South. Over time, the northern states outlawed slavery while the South continued to rely on slave labor. In 1854, Congress passed the Kansas-Nebraska Act, which gave these territories the power to determine if slavery would be allowed within their borders. This went against the 1820 Missouri Compromise. The act was met with anger by the North and support by the South.

Proslavery votes carried the majority, but the antislavery voters accused their opponents of fraud and did not accept the results. Instead,

All Men Are Created Equal

In 1776, the Founding Fathers of the United States intended to create a new nation built on the principles of freedom and equality. The Declaration of Independence states:

We hold these truths to be self-evident, that all men are created equal, that they are endowed by their Creator with certain unalienable Rights, that among these are Life, Liberty and the pursuit of Happiness.[1]

"All men," however, did not include blacks. Many people did not consider blacks to be equal to whites. Although George Washington had divided views on the issue of slavery, he was one of the largest slave owners in the country and supported the right of men to own slaves. Later in life, he changed his views. Jefferson, also a slave owner, did not believe people (white or black) were equal.

Nonetheless, the problem of slavery troubled these leaders. As educated men, they knew the system was morally wrong. But because slavery was so important in the South, they did not outlaw slavery in the US Constitution. Instead, they planned to limit it gradually. By the early 1800s, slavery was abolished in all northern states. As president in 1808, Jefferson signed a bill outlawing the slave trade, but slavery remained legal in 15 southern states and two territories until the end of the Civil War in 1865.

they held another election. This time, those who favored slavery did not vote, which resulted in the creation of two legislatures with opposing views. The issue of slavery from 1854 to 1858 erupted into such violence that the territory became known as Bleeding Kansas.

In 1861, when Lincoln announced slavery would be outlawed in new territories, the southern slaveholding states rebelled. These states believed Lincoln would attempt to end slavery where it already existed. As a result, most southern states seceded from the Union and formed the Confederate States of America.

In April 1861, the Civil War broke out between the Union army of the North and the Confederate army of the South. Lincoln's Emancipation Proclamation decreed that all slaves in rebellion territory were free as of January 1, 1863. Over four years, the war claimed 623,000 lives. In 1865, at the end of the war, Congress issued the

Sharecropping

The Civil War freed slaves but left them with few choices to earn a living. Lacking funds to buy their own farmland, thousands of former slaves resorted to a practice called share-cropping. Sharecroppers planted their crops on rented land. The landowners then took a percentage of the earnings. Usually, this percentage was so high that sharecroppers were unable to save any money, trapping them in the system for life. Children of sharecroppers rarely received any education because their help was needed on the farm. Instead of going to school, they worked. In the 1930s, poor sharecroppers began forming unions to protest the unfair system.

Thirteenth Amendment to the Constitution, which
formally abolished slavery.

Over the next several years, more laws were passed
to protect the rights of newly freed slaves. The Civil
Rights Act of 1866 guaranteed former slaves equality
before the law. The Fourteenth Amendment, passed
in 1868, declared blacks to have the full rights
of citizens except the right to vote. In 1870, the
Fifteenth Amendment guaranteed black males the
right to vote—although no women of any race were
allowed to vote. For the first time, African-American
men had the right to choose their leaders. Sixteen
blacks were voted into Congress.

A Nation Still Divided

Still, racist whites plotted ways to retain power.
In 1866, former Confederate soldiers formed the
Ku Klux Klan (KKK), a white supremacist group.
These men used terror tactics to stop blacks from
voting or asserting their rights. A common tactic was
to accuse blacks of a crime—whether or not the crime
had occurred. Those accused were often executed by
hanging, shooting, burning, or torture without their
cases being heard by a court of law. KKK members
and other white racists committed countless acts of

Ku Klux Klan members wore white hoods and sheets to represent the ghosts of Confederate Civil War soldiers seeking revenge.

brutality during the Reconstruction period when the North oversaw the rebuilding of the South.

White politicians also created rules making it more difficult for blacks to vote. For instance, black voters were required to take tests proving they could read. Whites did not have to take a test. In many areas, voters were required to pay a poll tax, which few blacks could afford. Some rules required that voters own property, which few blacks did. Denied their right to vote, southern blacks lost hope of equal rights.

A CHALLENGE

In 1876, racist whites in the South passed new laws that strictly segregated blacks and whites in almost every area of life. Blacks and whites could not attend the same schools, eat in the same restaurants, or even drink from the same water fountains. Public transportation was also segregated. Blacks rode on "colored" train cars and at the back of buses. These laws came to be known as the Jim Crow laws after a derogatory name used for black people.

In 1892, black activists in New Orleans, Louisiana, wanted to challenge the segregation laws. They chose a light-skinned black man, Homer Plessy, to board a train car for whites only. Plessy, a 30-year-old shoemaker and one-eighth black, was white in appearance. However,

Jim Crow Laws

From 1876 to 1965, Jim Crow laws segregated blacks and whites in the United States. According to one law, "The white and colored militia shall be separately enrolled, and shall never be compelled to serve in the same organization. The organization of colored troops shall not be permitted where white troops are available, and colored troops shall be under the command of white officers."[2]

racists considered that even one drop of black blood made a person black. When the conductor asked Plessy his race, he responded, "Colored."[3] The conductor ordered him off the whites-only car. When Plessy refused, he was arrested and jailed.

In court, Plessy's lawyers argued that the segregation of trains violated his rights under the Thirteenth and Fourteenth Amendments of the US Constitution. Judge John Howard Ferguson disagreed. Plessy appealed, and his case went to the US Supreme Court. In 1896, the Supreme Court decided the case of *Plessy v. Ferguson.* The court ruled segregation was legal as long as facilities for blacks and whites were equal in quality. This decision led to the policy of separate but equal segregation throughout the South. The policy remained for 58 years until *Brown v. Board of Education* outlawed segregation in schools.

Life in the North

Many blacks moved to northern cities to escape oppression in the South. However, they faced discrimination there as well. Unable to buy homes in white neighborhoods, they crowded into urban slums. They were not given equal opportunity for good schools or good jobs. This resulted in a standard of living that was, on average, far below that of white northerners.

Early Civil Rights Leaders

The US civil rights movement is usually defined as the period between 1955 and 1968 when mass numbers of people took direct action to fight for African-American rights. However, black people fought for their freedom from the time they were brought on slave ships to North American shores and continued to do so throughout US history. Early civil rights leaders included abolitionist Frederick Douglass. An escaped slave, he spoke and wrote against slavery. Harriet Tubman, who was born into slavery, risked her life to bring countless slaves to freedom in the North.

"I had reasoned [this] out in my mind; there was one of two things I had a *right* to, liberty, or death; if I could not have one, I would have [the other]."[4]
—*Harriet Tubman*

Booker T. Washington was a prominent black leader. In 1881, he founded Tuskegee Institute, a school for blacks, in Alabama. Washington taught blacks to uplift themselves through training and education. Ida B. Wells was an early activist. In the 1890s, she began speaking out against lynching and other unlawful executions of blacks in the South. A news reporter, she investigated hundreds of cases, finding that many of the victims who were lynched were innocent of any crime. Wells became famous in the United States and Europe for her activism against injustice.

In the early 1900s, black scholar W. E. B. DuBois emerged as a leader with a more aggressive civil rights plan. He criticized the federal government for being too accepting of white oppression and insisted that blacks must fight for their rights. In 1909, DuBois, along with Wells, helped found the National Association for the Advancement of Colored People (NAACP), an activist group that sought to combat racism in the courts.

In 1925, A. Philip Randolph introduced one of the first nationally recognized African-American labor organizations—the Brotherhood of Sleeping Car Porters. At the time, thousands of African Americans worked as porters on sleeping car trains across the United States. The labor union helped defend their rights and those of other black workers.

In 1941, as the United States entered World War II (1939–1945), blacks hoped to find jobs in the factories that made ships, tanks, and guns. However, because of racism, they were often restricted to sweeping and cleaning. Randolph successfully pressured President Franklin D. Roosevelt to pass

An Early Abolitionist

Frederick Douglass was born into slavery in 1818. His mother was a slave and his father was white. The master's wife taught young Frederick to read and write. At an early age, he read newspapers and followed the debate on slavery.

In 1838, Douglass escaped slavery. As a young man, he attended meetings in African-American churches and told of his experiences as a slave. An excellent, self-taught speaker, he advocated antislavery and gave speeches on the topic.

A supporter of women's suffrage, he participated in the first Women's Rights Convention in Seneca Falls in 1848. During the Civil War, he fought for the right for African Americans to enlist in the Union army.

Douglass, a former slave, abolitionist, newspaper editor, and civil rights activist, died on February 20, 1895.

a law banning job discrimination in government and in the defense industry. Years later, Randolph was one of the principal organizers of the 1963 March on Washington.

Thurgood Marshall, born in 1908, was a grandson of a slave. In 1930, he applied to the University of Maryland Law School. He was denied admission because he was black. This event had a profound effect on his future professional life. Marshall sought admission to and was accepted at the Howard University Law School. He became a lawyer and then a judge. In 1967, he was nominated and appointed to the US Supreme Court.

These early civil rights leaders and many more laid the groundwork for the civil rights movement of the 1950s and 1960s. This nonviolent revolution would shake the nation and change the course of history.

Abolitionist Frederick Douglass

Rosa Parks was arrested for not giving up her bus seat to a white person.

THE MONTGOMERY BUS BOYCOTT

On the evening of December 1, 1955, Rosa Parks boarded a city bus in Montgomery, Alabama. She was on her way home after a long day of work as a seamstress at a department store. As on all city buses in Montgomery, the front rows of seats were for whites only. Parks, an African American, obeyed the rules. She entered through the front door to pay her fare. She then got off the bus and entered again by the door that was to be used by colored people. She took a seat in the first row of seats in the middle of the bus for persons of color.

Soon, the bus began to fill up. One white man was left standing when the whites-only seats were all taken. The bus driver stepped over to the row where Parks and three other black people sat. "Y'all better make it light on yourselves and let me have those seats," the driver said.[1]

The three others stood up and moved, but Parks remained sitting. This was not the first time she had been treated unfairly on the buses, and she was tired of giving in. Parks responded that she did not think she had to move.

The bus driver warned her, "I'm going to have you arrested."

"You may do that," she replied.[2]

The driver stalked off the bus and returned shortly with two police officers. Parks was arrested and jailed for violating the segregation law.

"People always say that I didn't give up my seat because I was tired, but that isn't true. I was not tired physically, or no more tired than I usually was at the end of a working day. I was not old, although some people have an image of me as being old then. I was forty-two. No, the only tired I was, was tired of giving in."[3]

—*Rosa Parks*

"Stay Off the Buses"

News of Parks's arrest soon reached E. D. Nixon, a local civil rights leader. He had worked with Parks for the Montgomery branch of the NAACP. Nixon saw an opportunity. He and other activists had been fighting segregation on Montgomery's buses for a long time. If they could take her case to court and win, he thought they could force the city to change its laws forever.

Nixon bailed Parks out of jail and asked for her help in fighting the system. "With your permission," he said, "we can break down segregation on the bus with your case."[4] After

---

Challenging Segregation

Parks was not the first courageous woman to challenge segregation on public transport. A century earlier, in 1854, Elizabeth Jennings, a young black teacher, was brutally attacked and thrown out of a whites-only horse-drawn streetcar in New York City. Jennings sued the streetcar company for discrimination and won the case. As a result, all streetcars in New York City were desegregated.

Other brave black women challenged segregation. In 1944, Irene Morgan refused to move to the back of a bus traveling from Virginia to Maryland. Her case led to a US Supreme Court decision banning segregation in interstate commerce.

Claudette Colvin, Susie McDonald, Mary Louise Smith, and Aurelia Browder are not as well known as Parks, but they are just as important to the cause of civil rights. The question before the court was whether or not segregation of the Montgomery buses violated the Fourteenth Amendment of the US Constitution. The testimony of these young women in the case of *Browder v. Gayle* led to the end of segregation on buses in Montgomery.

---

talking to her husband and her mother, Parks agreed. The NAACP would take her case to court.

The next day, civil rights leaders in Montgomery sprang into action. In protest of Parks's arrest, the Women's Political Council (WPC) suggested holding a one-day boycott of the buses on the day of Parks's trial, December 5. African Americans made up nearly 75 percent of all riders on Montgomery's public buses. By refusing to ride the buses that day, they could send a clear message that they were no longer willing to cooperate with segregation laws.

Local ministers, including King and Ralph Abernathy, became involved in organizing the boycott. In a meeting at Dexter Baptist Church, where 26-year-old King was pastor, the details of the boycott were planned. Thousands of leaflets were printed and handed out. They read, in part:

> *Negroes have rights too. . . . Three-fourths of the riders are Negroes. We are . . . asking every Negro to stay off the buses Monday in protest of the arrest and trial. Don't ride the buses to work, to town, to school, or anywhere on Monday.*
>
> *You can afford to stay out of school for one day. . . . If you work, take a cab, or walk. But please, children and grownups, don't ride the bus at all on Monday.[5]*

*During the 381-day bus boycott,
many African Americans in Montgomery walked to work.*

Early Monday, December 5, King and his wife, Coretta Scott King, watched anxiously from their home. The first bus of the day was coming up the street. Typically, it was full of people on their way to work and school. But that day, it was empty. Bus after bus passed that morning, each was empty or had just a few passengers. Black people from all over the city walked, took cabs, and even rode mules rather than using the buses. The boycott was working.

New Face of the Movement

In court that day, Parks was found guilty and fined ten dollars plus court costs. She and her attorney, Fred Gray, filed an appeal.

Civil rights activists formed a new organization called the Montgomery Improvement Association (MIA). Their first act was to elect King as president of the organization. He would lead the MIA as it continued the bus boycott and other protests against segregation on Montgomery buses.

King knew the job was dangerous. Undoubtedly, whoever led the movement would be the focus of the racists' anger and could be targeted for violence. But the young minister accepted the leadership role without hesitation.

That evening, King spoke at the Holt Baptist Church before a gathering of 5,000 people. Many did not know who he was, but after his speech, no one would forget him. He spoke to the crowd,

> There comes a time when people get tired. We are here this evening to say to those who have mistreated us so long that we are tired, tired of being segregated and humiliated, tired of being kicked about by the brutal feet of oppression. . . . That is our challenge and overwhelming responsibility.[6]

He emphasized, however, that as angry as the people were, they could not resort to violence:

> In our protest there will be no cross burnings; no white person will be taken from his home by a hooded Negro mob and brutally murdered . . . we will be guided by the highest principles of law and order. Once again we must hear the words of Jesus, "Love your enemies. Bless them that curse you."[7]

The bus boycott continued for more than a year. The MIA helped by organizing carpools for the thousands of people who needed transportation. The boycott did not go unnoticed. The bus company lost more than half of its income, and businesses in Montgomery suffered because blacks no longer took the buses to shop downtown.

White business owners, city leaders, and whites who opposed desegregation became angry. Many who participated in the boycott lost their jobs. Parks was fired shortly after her arrest and had no steady work for a year. The police arrested King and other leaders for

Nonviolent Protest

King believed deeply in the power of nonviolent protest to bring about social change. He felt African Americans could not win their rights by resorting to violence. Although white racists often used terror tactics such as bombs and lynchings, King continually emphasized the need for blacks to fight hate with love.

organizing the boycott. However, the riders refused to give in until the city met their demand to end segregation on Montgomery's buses for good.

> "Darkness cannot drive out darkness; only light can do that. Hate cannot drive out hate; only love can do that."[8]
> —*Martin Luther King Jr.*

Through his leadership of the boycott, King had become the face of the American civil rights movement. He appeared in magazines and newspapers all over the world. In January 1956, King's house was bombed. His wife and their baby daughter were inside, but no one was harmed. Hearing of the bombing, an angry crowd of King's supporters gathered in front of his home. Some held weapons and plotted revenge. King came out on the front porch to talk to the crowd. As always, he argued that they must not return violence with violence. Later, white racists also bombed four black churches and the homes of Nixon and Abernathy.

Victory in the Courts

Parks's lawyer had filed an appeal on her behalf, but they knew the case could be tied up in the courts for years. Nixon and other NAACP leaders searched for another way to challenge the segregation law. They found four more women in Montgomery who had been victims of discrimination on the buses: Claudette Colvin, Susie McDonald, Mary Louise Smith, and Aurelia Browder. In February 1956, the four women filed a lawsuit arguing that segregation on buses violated their constitutional rights. Their case, *Browder v. Gayle*, made it to the US Supreme Court. In November 1956, the court ruled that segregation on buses within a state was unconstitutional.

The bus boycott ended the next day. When blacks in Montgomery rode the buses again, they sat side by side with white passengers. It had been a major victory for civil rights.

A New Beginning

In January 1957, African-American ministers formed the Southern Christian Leadership Conference (SCLC). King was named president of the organization that would organize civil rights demonstrations all over the South.

The bus boycott had shown African Americans they could stand up for their rights and win. Over the next decade, many more battles would be fought and won in the US civil rights movement.

King became the face of the civil rights movement.

1954 Public School Segregation

State Segregation Policy

Required by law Determined by local law Prohibited by law Not legislated

In 1954, before the Supreme Court's ruling on Brown v. Board of Education, segregation was legally required in 17 southern states and Washington DC.

CRISIS IN LITTLE ROCK

While King led the 381-day protest against bus segregation in Montgomery, many other deeply ingrained aspects of life in the South continued to be segregated by race. One of these included education.

On May 17, 1954, the US Supreme Court ruled
in *Brown v. Board of Education*. In this landmark case,
segregation in schools was declared unconstitutional.
This decision required all public schools in the
United States to integrate. After the *Brown* decision,
a few southern states began to integrate right away,
but others ignored the Supreme Court ruling. White
segregationists vowed to fight the law. They believed
blacks and whites should be separated and resented
the federal government intervening in what they
thought of as the southern way of life.

Southern politicians used many tactics to delay
integration, including closing schools rather than
integrating them. In Prince Edward County,
Virginia, the public schools were closed for five
years. During that time, white students were sent
to special private schools, and many black children
received no education at all. With these tactics, it
looked as though white segregationists might never
comply with federal law.

The Little Rock Nine

The conflict over school desegregation escalated
into a national crisis in Little Rock, Arkansas. The
NAACP had pushed hard for integration. At last, in

1957, the Arkansas school board agreed to integrate a public high school in Little Rock, the state's capital.

A group of nine black students were chosen for their excellent grades and attendance records. These students registered at the Little Rock Central High School in September. The Little Rock Nine, as they became known, were Ernest Green, Elizabeth Eckford, Jefferson Thomas, Terrence Roberts, Carlotta Walls, Minnijean Brown, Gloria Ray, Thelma Mothershed, and Melba Pattillo.

Separate but Unequal

According to the 1896 Supreme Court ruling in *Plessy v. Ferguson*, states could maintain separate schools for whites and blacks as long as the schools were equal in quality. In reality, most segregated schools were far from equal. Black schools often lacked books and other supplies because most of the funding for education went to white schools. School buildings for blacks were generally inferior, and the playgrounds and bathrooms were in poor condition. Another issue was that superior white schools were often closer to the blacks' homes than a separate but equal school for blacks.

The original *Brown v. Board of Education* case involved schools in Topeka, Kansas. By the time the case reached the Supreme Court in 1954, it included cases from Kansas, South Carolina, Virginia, and Delaware. Chief Justice Earl Warren's court determined that the doctrine of separate but equal had no place in public education. The court also ruled that the rights of African Americans, as stated in the Fourteenth Amendment, were violated. Members of the court agreed that even if the teachers and the facilities for segregated schools were of equal quality, segregation was harmful to black students and unconstitutional. The court's unanimous decision overturned the separate but equal ruling in *Plessy v. Ferguson*.

September 4 was the first day of school. On that day, 15-year-old Elizabeth wore a dress she and her mother had made for the occasion. Elizabeth was excited and a bit nervous. She knew some students might be unfriendly to her. Still, she was determined to attend Central, which she knew was a very good school. As her family sat down to breakfast, Elizabeth's brother turned on the television. The announcer was talking about a large crowd that had gathered at the school. The news upset Elizabeth's mother.

For safety reasons, the other eight black students had arranged to be driven to school by Daisy Bates, president of the Arkansas chapter of the NAACP. Elizabeth had not received the message, so she took the city bus. As she stepped off the bus, an angry mob of white people began shouting threats and racial insults. Keeping her head high, she hurried to the front of the school where a line of National Guard troops stood holding bayonets.

The Ugly Face of Racism

Years after they were confronted by the angry mob in front of Central High School on September 4, 1957, the Little Rock Nine clearly recalled the ugly racism they had seen on that day. "I tried to see a friendly face somewhere in the mob—someone who maybe would help," remembered Elizabeth. "I looked into the face of an old woman and it seemed a kind face, but when I looked at her again, she spat on me."[1]

Terrence remembered that the protestors "ranged in age from very young to very old. . . . And the words that came out of their mouths were shocking. They really wanted to kill us."[2]

If she could get to the guards, she knew they would protect her. But when Elizabeth reached the front door, the guards only glared at her. She tried to move past them to enter the school, but they blocked her. She realized the armed guards were not there to protect her. Like the rest of the mob, they were there to keep her from entering. As she stood not knowing what to do, someone began to yell, "Lynch her! Lynch her!"[3] Elizabeth fled in terror and ran back to the bus stop.

Meanwhile, the other eight students arrived by car. They, too, were prevented from entering the school by the guards. The first day of school had been a disaster for the Little Rock Nine.

A Governor's Standoff

The eyes of the nation were on Little Rock. Arkansas Governor Orval Faubus had ordered 250 National Guard troops to be posted outside Central High School.

By standing in the way of integration, Faubus disobeyed a federal law. On September 20, under federal court order, the mayor was forced to call off the guardsmen. Three days later, on September 23, the nine black students approached the school

City and state police guard Central High School in Little Rock, Arkansas, on September 23, 1957, as the school was desegregated.

again—escorted by Little Rock police officers. The situation was dangerous. A crowd of more than 1,000 people outside the school became enraged when they learned the students were inside. On the street, news reporters and black passersby were attacked and beaten. Police were losing control and feared a riot. Melba remembered:

I'd only been in the school a couple of hours and by this time it was apparent that the mob was just overrunning the school. . . . We were trapped. And I thought, Okay, so I'm going to die here, in school. . . . A couple of the kids, the black kids, that were with me were crying, and someone made a suggestion that if they allowed the mob to hang one kid, they could get the rest out.[4]

Fortunately, none of the students were harmed that day. Police were able to get them out of the school by using a side door and drove them out through the mob.

Looking for Votes

Faubus claimed the guards were at Central to preserve the peace and avert violence that would surely result if the black students were allowed in the school. "Blood will run in the streets," he had warned the day before.[5] However, Faubus also had political reasons to stop the school from being integrated. He was up for reelection the following year and needed the segregationists' votes.

The next day, the mayor of Little Rock sent a telegram to Washington asking for help from the federal government. President Dwight D. Eisenhower responded by taking command of the 10,000 soldiers of the Arkansas National Guard and sending 1,000 US Army paratroopers from the 101st Airborne Division to Little Rock. On September 25, 1957, paratroopers stood guard around the school and helicopters hovered overhead as the nine students entered Little Rock Central High School.

CRACKING THE WALL

Once the black students entered school, new troubles began. While many of their classmates were friendly to them, the black students still faced daily harassment and hostility. They were tripped, shoved, and called names. Their lockers were vandalized and their belongings were stolen.

The constant abuse wore the students down. Knowing they would be blamed for causing the trouble, they dared not retaliate. Then one day in December, a boy followed Minnijean through the cafeteria, taunting her with a racial slur. Minnijean had heard the word many times before, but this time, she was fed up. She picked up her bowl of chili and dumped it on the boy's head. After a moment of stunned silence, the cafeteria workers, who were African American, broke into applause.

Minnijean was suspended from school. Later, in February, she was expelled for insulting a girl who used similar abusive language. For the segregationists, this was a victory.

"I worried about silly things, like keeping my saddle shoes straight, what am I going to wear today—things that a fifteen-year-old girl does worry about, but also which part of the hall to walk in that's the safest. Who's going to hit me with what? Is it going to be hot soup today? Is it going to be so greasy that it ruins the dress my grandmother made for me? How's this day going to go?"[6]

—*Melba Pattillo of the Little Rock Nine*

They passed out cards at the high school reading ONE DOWN . . . EIGHT TO GO. Their boasting was in vain as the remaining eight students stayed for the entire year.

In the spring, Ernest became the first black student to graduate from Little Rock Central High. The event not only received national attention, but King attended the ceremony. "When I walked across the stage, no one clapped," Ernest recalled years later. "But, you know, I felt good anyway. I had cracked the wall and others would come through it."[7]

Still, the fight was not over. During the summer, Faubus pushed new laws through that allowed him to close the schools rather than continue with desegregation. White segregationists continued to delay integration in schools throughout the South. But Little Rock had proved they could not delay forever. The extraordinary courage of nine young students inspired thousands of others to continue the fight until all schools were finally integrated. —

THE LITTLE ROCK NINE

The first black students at Central High School in Little Rock, Arkansas, became known as the Little Rock Nine.

In February 1960, African Americans began a sit-in at Woolworth's lunch counter.

SIT-INS AND FREEDOM RIDES

On February 1, 1960, four young black men sat at a Woolworth's lunch counter in Greensboro, North Carolina. However, they were not eating lunch. The waitress had told them, "We don't serve you here."[1]

The young men, freshmen at North Carolina Agricultural and Technical College in Greensboro, politely disagreed. They showed the waitress their receipts from other purchases in the store. They wanted to know why Woolworth's would serve black people at one counter and deny them service at another.

The waitress did not have an answer. Instead, she called the store manager. He asked the four teenagers to leave, but they remained in their seats. Soon, a policeman entered the store. Angry at the sight of black people at a whites-only lunch counter, he paced the aisle behind them, hitting his club against his hand. The four young men remained sitting peacefully at the counter. As they had not broken any law, the officer had no reason to arrest them. "You had the feeling he didn't know what . . . to do," recalled one of the students, Franklin McCain. "You had the feeling that this is the first time

The First Sit-ins

The first sit-ins were organized in Chicago, Illinois, in 1942 by the Congress of Racial Equality (CORE). This group succeeded in desegregating a number of restaurants in the Chicago area, but the movement did not spread to other regions.

In 1958, a group of students with the NAACP Youth Council desegregated several restaurants in Oklahoma City. Sit-ins were also staged in several other cities in Oklahoma and Kansas.

However, it was not until the Greensboro sit-in that the movement really took off. As student Diane Nash reflected, "We started feeling the power of an idea whose time had come."[2]

that this big bad man with the gun and the club has been pushed in a corner."[3]

The students stayed for another half hour until the store closed. McCain stated,

If it's possible to know what it means to have your soul cleansed—I felt pretty clean at that time. . . . I felt as though I had gained my manhood. . . . Not Franklin McCain only as an individual, but I felt as though the manhood of a number of other black persons had been restored and had gotten some respect from just that one day.[4]

A Stark Contrast

Several months before the first Greensboro sit-in, a group of students in Nashville, Tennessee, had planned their own sit-ins. They had gone through nonviolence training and learned how to ignore harassment without fighting back. On February 27, 1960, the group's training was put to the test as their peaceful sit-in at a Nashville Woolworth's turned violent. A gang of young white men poured ketchup and mustard on the heads of the black students, stubbed out cigarettes on their backs, and beat and kicked some of them. The students remained in their seats. When police arrived to quell the disturbance, they arrested the peaceful student protestors—and not the racist gang—for disorderly conduct. The incident disgusted many Americans, who learned about it on television and in newspapers. In May 1960, Nashville's mayor, Ben West, called for desegregation in the city's restaurants.

The students' commitment to nonviolence was the key to the success of the sit-ins. Even as onlookers shouted insults or shoved and hit them, the protestors remained calm. They kept their eyes down and avoided confrontation by studying their textbooks. The stark contrast between the crude, thuggish behavior of the white racists and the polite, restrained demeanor of the students created public sympathy for the students and their cause.

The four students, McCain, David Richmond, Joseph McNeil, and Ezell Blair Jr., did not yet know it, but their simple act of defiance would turn into a movement and spread throughout the South.

A Student Movement

The Greensboro Four, as they became known, were part of a new generation of student activists. Only 12 or 13 years old in 1955 when the Montgomery bus boycott began, they had grown up hearing about King and the fight for civil rights. They had studied the writings of India's independence leader Mohandas Gandhi and his concept of nonviolent resistance. Impatient for change, they felt it was time for young people to take a stand against injustice.

The day after their first sit-in, the Greensboro Four returned to the lunch counter with more than

A New Way

In a statement of support for student activists in Atlanta, Georgia, President John F. Kennedy said, "[You] have shown that the new way for Americans to stand up for their rights is to sit down."[5]

20 classmates. On the following day, the group had grown to more than 60. By the end of the week, more than 300 students participated, including white students from a local women's college. The students worked in shifts, taking turns so that all of the lunch counter seats were occupied all day long. They expanded their protest to include other stores in Greensboro. Nonviolence was key to the sit-ins. If the students were hit, they did not strike back.

The demonstrations attracted attention. As reporters and angry crowds gathered, word spread to other colleges. Within a week, students held sit-ins in North Carolina, South Carolina, and Virginia. By the end of February, student protests took place in more than 30 cities across the South. The movement continued to grow. Students began targeting any place that prohibited blacks, including libraries, swimming pools, churches, and movie theaters. Their goal was to defeat segregation.

Approximately six months after the sit-in at the Woolworth's lunch counter in Greensboro, the store owners had lost so much business due to the protests. They had no choice but to integrate. On July 25, 1960, African Americans were served for the first time at the lunch counter in Greensboro's

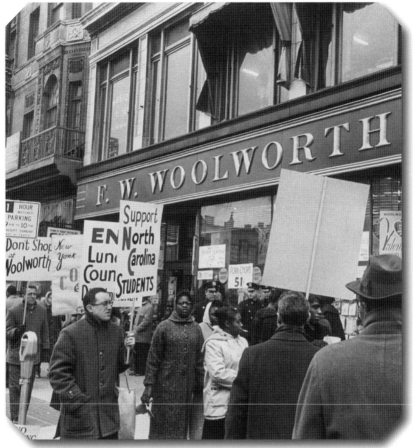

Demonstrators in Harlem, New York, supported the desegregation sit-ins in the South.

Woolworth's. The following day, all Woolworth's stores in the country were open to black customers. By the end of the year, lunch counters were desegregated in at least 80 other southern cities.

Riding for Freedom

In April 1960, student activists created the Student Nonviolent Coordinating Committee (SNCC, pronounced "snick"). After the success of the sit-ins, the next injustice that students wanted to tackle was the issue of segregation on interstate buses.

In 1946, the US Supreme Court had ruled segregation on interstate transport unconstitutional. In 1960, it also outlawed segregation in bus terminals. But as blacks traveling through the South knew all too well, the law was not enforced. There were still black waiting rooms and black lunch counters in bus terminals in Mississippi, Alabama, Georgia, and elsewhere in the South. Blacks were expected to sit in the back of the buses that traveled through these areas. SNCC, working with CORE, decided it was time to force the segregationists to follow federal law.

On May 4, 1961, a group of 13 Freedom Riders— seven blacks and six whites—from CORE and SNCC boarded two buses leaving from Washington DC and heading to New Orleans. Lewis, one of the protestors at the Nashville sit-ins, was among the Freedom Riders. The whites and blacks sat next to each other on the buses and at bus terminal facilities,

ignoring the signs that said WHITES ONLY. As they
headed deeper into the South, they encountered
trouble. Two riders, one white and one black, were
beaten by a white gang when they tried to enter a
whites-only waiting room together. The next day,
another two riders were jailed.

When the buses reached Alabama, a stronghold
of the KKK, the true horror began. A mob of angry
whites had heard about the Freedom Riders and
waited at the Anniston, Alabama, bus terminal.
The mob attacked one of the buses,
breaking windows and slashing tires.
A fire bomb was tossed through
a window. As passengers tried
frantically to escape, the mob held
the doors shut. Fortunately, the
riders were able to get out just before
the bus exploded into flames. When
another bus arrived in Birmingham,
another mob of Klansmen beat the
Freedom Riders. William Barbee was
so badly beaten that he was paralyzed
for life. Police in Birmingham,
who allied with the Klan, did not
intervene to stop any of the violence.

No Sympathy

The governor of Alabama,
John Patterson, had no
sympathy for the riders.
"When you go looking
for trouble, you usually
find it."[6]

On May 24, 1961, James Farmer, director of CORE, sat at an all-white lunch counter in Montgomery before a bus of Freedom Riders left.

"Willing to Accept Death"

After the violence in Alabama, CORE leader James Farmer wanted to stop the Freedom Rides. But SNCC insisted it must continue or the racists would think they had won. A second group of ten students was selected to travel to Birmingham to continue the Freedom Ride. They knew the potential dangers of the ride. "We were informed we should be willing to accept death," said Susan Herman, who had chosen to join the ride.[7]

President Kennedy had monitored the situation and was reluctant to intervene, knowing it would impact his popularity in the South. However, he sent one of his aides, John Seigenthaler, to speak with Governor Patterson, who promised police protection for the riders. On May 20, the riders began their journey from Birmingham to Montgomery. Once in Montgomery, the police disappeared—and another vicious mob attacked. Knocked unconscious, Seigenthaler was among those who were assaulted. The president was forced to act. He sent 600 federal troops to Alabama to protect the Freedom Riders, who were mobbed at the hospital where they were being treated.

In the midst of the crisis, King flew to Montgomery to speak at a rally held at the First Baptist Church. When it grew dark, a mob laid siege to the church, shouting curses, burning cars, and throwing rocks. The people inside were trapped and terrified for their lives. King told them,

> *We are not going to become panicky. We are going to be calm, and . . . continue to stand up for what we know is right. . . . We are not afraid and we shall overcome.*[8]

Under pressure from the president, Patterson declared martial law in the state of Alabama. He sent out the National Guard and state police to disperse the mobs.

On May 24, the Freedom Riders continued their journey under the protection of the Alabama National Guard. This time, there were no mobs and no violence. When they arrived in Mississippi, however, they were arrested and put into prison for 60 days for violating state segregation laws.

Still, nothing would stop the Freedom Rides. By the end of the summer, more than 300 riders had joined the movement. As one group of riders was arrested, others took their places on the buses. In November 1961, under orders from President Kennedy, new regulations were made to enforce integration on interstate buses and in bus terminals.

Dedication

Jim Zwerg, a white Freedom Rider, was severely beaten in Montgomery. He stated, "Segregation must be stopped. It must be broken down . . . we are dedicated to this. We will take hitting. We'll take beatings. We're willing to accept death. But we are going to keep coming until we can ride anywhere in the South . . . as Americans."[9]

African-American Freedom Riders were arrested in Jackson, Mississippi.

*Birmingham's Public Safety Commissioner Bull Connor
oversaw the arrest of African-American demonstrators in April 1963.*

THE BIRMINGHAM
CAMPAIGN

*I*n 1961, Freedom Riders traveling
through Birmingham had been mobbed
and brutally beaten. Birmingham's public safety
commissioner, T. Eugene "Bull" Connor, was a
notorious racist and KKK supporter. The police,

under orders from Connor, looked the other way.
Even the governor of Alabama had failed to protect
the civil rights activists, showing that the system of
hate extended to the highest levels.

In 1962, students led protests against segregation
in the city's department stores. However, the city
refused to negotiate with them. In November 1962,
Connor ran for mayor of Birmingham. He lost to
Albert Boutwell, who was only somewhat less of a
combative segregationist.

By 1963, Birmingham was known as one of the
most segregated cities in the South. Approximately
40 percent of its people were African American.
However, they were not treated as equal citizens.
So many acts of violence had been committed
against blacks in Birmingham that newspapers
nicknamed the city "Bombingham."[1] In the spring
of 1963, King announced it was time for civil rights
activists to launch "a full-scale assault" in the city of
Birmingham.[2]

Project C

King was determined to carefully plan the
Birmingham project, which he called Project C for
confrontation. The previous year, he had helped lead

a similar campaign in Albany, Georgia, but he left in defeat after months of protest had brought little change. This time, he did not want to fail. In the spring of 1963, King and other SCLC leaders met with Reverend Fred Shuttlesworth, a minister and activist in Birmingham. They created a detailed plan for major citywide protests.

The protests began on April 3, 1963, in downtown Birmingham. Protestors staged sit-ins at segregated lunch counters. Stores responded by closing their lunch counters. Three days later, on April 6, protestors marched to Birmingham's city hall and were arrested. The next day, the protestors marched again. This time, police attacked with nightsticks and police dogs. On Wednesday, April 10, the leaders, including King, Shuttlesworth, and Abernathy, were ordered by the Alabama circuit court not to take part in any more demonstrations. Connor was trying to shut them down.

King made a decision to continue the demonstrations and face the consequences. On Friday, April 12, King led another march on city hall and was arrested and jailed. While in solitary confinement, he wrote his "Letter from a Birmingham Jail." The letter was an explanation

In April 1963, Abernathy, left, and King, right, were arrested after participating in a demonstration in Birmingham.

of what he and his fellow protestors were trying to accomplish in Birmingham:

You may well ask, "Why direct action? Why sit-ins, marches, and so forth? Isn't negotiation a better path?" . . . Indeed, this is the very purpose of direct action . . . to create such a crisis and foster such a tension that a community which has constantly refused to negotiate is forced to confront the issue. It seeks so to dramatize the issue that it can no longer be ignored. . . . The purpose of our direct-action program is to create a situation so crisis-packed that it will inevitably open the door to negotiation.[3]

King's arrest made national news. Now all eyes were on Birmingham, waiting to see what would happen next.

THE CHILDREN'S CRUSADE

Once King was released from jail, he planned the next stage of the Birmingham campaign: a mass march of Birmingham schoolchildren. On Thursday, May 2, they gathered at the Sixteenth Street Baptist Church and began to march toward downtown. Police arrested marchers by the wagonload, but more kept on

The Wait

King's "Letter from a Birmingham Jail" has become one of his most famous pieces of writing. In it, he expressed the pain and frustration felt by many African Americans during the civil rights struggle. "For years now, I have heard the word 'Wait,'" King wrote. He continued:

This "Wait" has almost always meant "Never.". . . Perhaps it is easy for those who have never felt the stinging darts of segregation to say "Wait." But when you have seen vicious mobs lynch your mothers and fathers at will and drown your sisters and brothers at whim; when you have seen hate-filled policemen curse, kick, and even kill your black brothers and sisters; when you see the vast majority of your twenty million Negro brothers smothering in an airtight cage of poverty in the midst of an affluent society, when you suddenly find your tongue twisted and your speech stammering as you seek to explain to your six-year-old daughter why she can't go to the public amusement park that has just been advertised on television, and see tears welling up in her eyes when she is told that Funtown is closed to colored children, and see ominous clouds of inferiority beginning to form in her little mental sky . . . then you will understand why we find it difficult to wait.[4]

marching. By the end of the day, 959 students, aged six to eighteen, were in jail.

The following day, May 3, more than 1,000 children skipped school to join in the march. This time, Connor retaliated with force. He brought out police dogs and ordered firefighters to turn their hoses on the children. The high-pressure hoses that were strong enough to rip the bark off trees knocked children off their feet. Dogs tore at the children's clothing. As the protests continued for several more days, the masses of marchers increased. The entire black community was angry, and they took their anger into the streets.

Across the nation and all over the world, television news broadcasted pictures of children being brutalized by dogs and fire hoses. Viewers were shocked and disgusted. President Kennedy felt the incident was an embarrassment for the United States. Denouncing Connor's actions as "shameful," the president sent officials to help resolve the crisis.[5] Birmingham's white business owners, who had lost weeks of business, agreed to a settlement. They would desegregate all lunch counters, bathrooms, fitting rooms, and water fountains. They also agreed to begin hiring black employees.

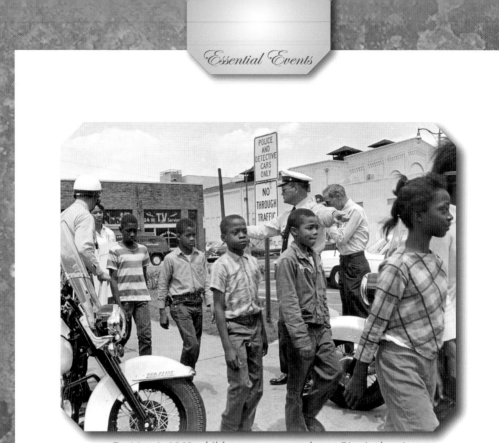

On May 4, 1963, children were arrested near Birmingham's city hall for protesting racial discrimination.

A settlement was reached, but the trouble in Birmingham was not over yet. A day later, bombs exploded at King's hotel and at the home of his brother, Birmingham minister A. D. King. No one was hurt, but his home was ruined. Angry protests ensued with more police brutality. On May 13, President Kennedy stationed federal troops outside the city, and the violence stopped. The Birmingham campaign was over. It appeared as though the civil rights leaders had won.

A Nation at War with Itself

As spring turned to summer, the United States seemed to be going through a second civil war. Across the country, African Americans took to the streets. They held sit-ins and marches. In Georgia, Virginia, Maryland, Alabama, and even in Harlem, New York, protests turned bloody as police retaliated, using fire hoses, tear gas, and nightsticks to break up civil rights demonstrations. On June 11, 1963, NAACP leader Medgar Evers was murdered in Jackson, Mississippi.

In response to the national upheaval, the president drafted new civil rights legislation, which would become the Civil Rights Act of 1964. While the nation awaited the outcome of the bill by a bitterly divided Congress, civil rights organizers decided the time was right to bring their protests to Washington DC. The March on Washington for Jobs and

Death Threats

As a leader of the Mississippi NAACP, Evers received death threats daily. When he returned home on June 11, 1963, Klan member Byron de la Beckwith was waiting. Beckwith shot Evers in the back with a high-powered hunting rifle, which he left at the scene. Evers died later that night at the hospital. Police found the weapon with Beckwith's fingerprints and arrested him.

In 1964, despite strong evidence, the trial ended in a mistrial. A second trial also ended in a mistrial. In both trials, all-white juries failed to convict Beckwith. The case was reopened in 1989. In his third trial, Beckwith was convicted and sentenced to life in prison where he died in 2001.

Freedom took place on August 28, 1963.

Just weeks after the historic demonstration, violence struck again. The Sixteenth Street Baptist Church in Birmingham was used for civil rights meetings. On September 15, 1963, a bomb went off at the church. Four little girls were killed. The dream of equality was still far from reach.

Freedom

On April 16, 1963, in a letter from the Birmingham jail, King wrote, "Freedom is never voluntarily given by the oppressor; it must be demanded by the oppressed."[6]

On September 15, 1963, the Sixteenth Street Baptist Church
in Birmingham was bombed.

On July 2, 1964, Johnson signed the Civil Rights Act of 1964 and gave one of the pens to King.

THE RIGHT TO VOTE

O n November 22, 1963, President Kennedy was assassinated in Dallas, Texas. Approximately two hours later, as the nation mourned, Vice President Lyndon Johnson took the oath of office aboard Air Force One in Dallas.

Five days later, Johnson addressed Congress:

. . . no memorial oration or eulogy could more eloquently honor President Kennedy's memory than the earliest possible passage of the Civil Rights Bill for which he fought so long. We have talked long enough in this country about equal rights. We have talked for a hundred years or more. Yes, it is time now to write the next chapter—and to write it in books of law. . . . I urge you . . . to enact a civil rights law.[1]

Under Johnson's leadership, the Civil Rights Act was passed on July 2, 1964. Often described as the most sweeping civil rights legislation since the Reconstruction era, the Civil Rights Act prohibits discrimination in employment and federally assisted programs and outlaws segregation in public places.

Voting Rights

Major obstacles still stood in the way of African-American equality— one of which was voting rights. The Fifteenth Amendment had granted former male slaves the right to vote in 1870. But nearly 100 years later, blacks across the South were routinely blocked from voting.

A Start

The passage of the Civil Rights Act was a historic event. African Americans now had more job opportunities, the voting laws were strengthened, and funding was limited to aid programs that were discriminatory. Still, all of the issues of discrimination were not resolved.

White racists used a variety of tactics to keep black people from voting. Black voters were forced to take difficult literacy tests that were purposely written to be impossible to pass. The voter registration forms they were given were long and complex. Many times, the door to the voter registration office was shut in their faces. Some blacks who attempted to register were threatened, harassed, and beaten. They risked losing their jobs, their homes, or even their lives.

Mississippi was the state with the worst record regarding voting rights. Civil rights volunteers had worked there for nearly three years, yet only 5 percent of voting-age blacks were registered to vote. This was not because they were uninterested in voting. It was because they were afraid. But without the power to choose their own representatives in government, African Americans could never demand justice. In the summer of 1964, civil rights workers concentrated their energies on Mississippi in a massive voter registration drive.

Mississippi Freedom Summer

Robert Moses, a young African-American math teacher from New York, led the voting rights campaign that is known as Mississippi Freedom

Summer. Beginning in 1961, Moses went door-to-door in Mississippi with groups of student volunteers from SNCC, encouraging blacks to register to vote. In 1962, the NAACP, SCLC, and CORE joined forces with SNCC to form the Council of Federated Organizations (COFO). The COFO recruited approximately 800 college students from all over the country to join the campaign.

Most of these young volunteers were white students from schools such as Harvard and Berkeley. Before departing for Mississippi, they participated in an intense training program to help prepare them for the hostility they would face. The volunteers were also told they risked being injured or killed.

On June 21, 1964, the first day of Mississippi Freedom Summer, three volunteers were reported missing. Their bodies were found 44 days later buried at a construction site. Throughout that summer, white racists continued to terrorize the

Robert Moses

Although an important civil rights leader, Moses did not seek the spotlight. Soft-spoken and with a spiritual air, he preferred to be seen as one of many members of a collective movement rather than as a spokesperson. Moses grew up in a poor neighborhood in Harlem, but he attended an elite public high school and studied at Harvard for his PhD. When his father became ill, he quit school and became a math teacher. In 1960, Moses joined SNCC and became one of the group's most hardworking and effective organizers.

Mississippi Burning

On June 21, 1964, three civil rights volunteers working in Mississippi, two of whom were white, investigated a church burning. Andrew Goodman, 20, Michael Schwerner, 24, and James Chaney, 21, were arrested and thrown in jail. Well after nightfall, they were released by the sheriff. Then they disappeared. The story made national news, and the FBI began a secret investigation, code-named Mississippi Burning. In August, an informant led agents to a construction site where the bodies were buried. The young men had been kidnapped and shot by KKK members in league with the sheriff. Eighteen men, including the sheriff, were charged. Only seven were convicted, and none served more than six years in jail.

civil rights activists with false arrests, beatings, shootings, burnings, and bombings. But the onslaught of violence made the volunteers even more determined to stay and fight. That summer, the volunteers set up Mississippi Freedom Schools for black Americans to supplement their inferior education. Not only children, but people of all ages, attended the schools. As the black citizens learned more about their political rights, they were more determined to stand up for them.

Mississippi Freedom

One of the main goals of the Mississippi Freedom Summer was to give African Americans a voice in politics. Since black people were not welcomed to join the Republican and Democratic Parties in Mississippi, the activists formed the Mississippi Freedom Democratic Party (MFDP). By the end of the summer, they had signed up 63,000 black voters as members of the new party. Now, they were ready to challenge the all-white Democratic Party.

In August 1964, MFDP delegates traveled to Atlantic City, New Jersey, to attend the Democratic National Convention. Thirty-four delegates, or representatives, from Mississippi's Democratic Party attended the convention. All of these representatives were white. The MFDP argued that this was unfair and insisted African Americans be included. Delegate Fannie Lou Hamer gave a televised speech before the committee. She related her struggles as a black woman to get the right to vote. She described how she and other women had been jailed and beaten for attempting to vote in Mississippi:

> *They beat me and they beat me with the long, flat blackjack. I screamed to God in pain. My dress worked itself up. I tried to pull it down. They beat my arms 'til I had no feeling in them. . . . If the Freedom Democratic Party is not seated now, I question America. Is [this] America, the land of the free and the home of the brave . . . ?*[2]

For the first time, viewers across the nation heard of the brutal way blacks' votes were being suppressed. Many at the convention called for the MFDP delegates to be included. The Democrats offered a compromise: the black delegates could have two seats but no voting rights in the convention. The delegates rejected the compromise and went home in defeat.

"We didn't come all this way for no two seats," Hamer said in disgust.[3]

Bloody Sunday

In January 1965, King arrived in Selma, Alabama, to help with SNCC voter registration drives. As in Mississippi and elsewhere in the South, white resistance was strong. Peaceful protestors marched together to the courthouse, singing freedom songs. They waited in line hour after hour, knowing the door would never open for them. They took the literacy tests and were told they had failed. Time and again, protestors were arrested and jailed, including King. In February, a young, black army veteran, Jimmy Lee Jackson, was shot and killed by state troopers during a peaceful march.

On Sunday, March 7, King planned a march of 54 miles (87 km) from Selma to the state capitol in Montgomery. Governor George Wallace, a segregationist, banned the demonstration, but the activists ignored his order. They expected they could be jailed, but what happened was far worse. As the protestors crossed the Edmund Pettus Bridge in Selma, they were met by state troopers. When the marchers did not retreat, the troopers sprayed them with tear gas, knocked them down, and beat them. Civil rights organizer Lewis was clubbed in the head. As he fell to the ground, he recalled thinking, "This is it . . . I'm going to die here."[5]

No one died that day, but many were seriously injured. The scenes, shown on television that evening, "looked like war," recalled the mayor of Selma.[6] The day became known as Bloody Sunday.

STILL MARCHING

In the following days and weeks, demonstrations were held in more than 80 cities in protest of the violence. King staged more marches in Selma. On March 9, a second march to Montgomery ended when troops again stood guard at the bridge. That evening, James Reeb, a minister, was struck on the head with a club and died several days later. On March 21, approximately 25,000 people participated in a third march from Selma to Montgomery. This time, they reached Montgomery. However, their joy was dampened when they learned of another death. Viola Liuzzo, a white volunteer from Detroit, Michigan, had been shot and killed by the KKK.

On August 6, almost five months after the marches in Selma, President Johnson signed the Voting Rights Act of 1965. The law banned literacy tests and other voting requirements. It allowed the federal government to supervise elections in states that refused voter registration. With federal government oversight, millions of African Americans throughout the South cast their first ballots that fall. ⌒

"Today I want to say . . . we are not about to turn around. We are on the move now. . . . We are moving to the land of freedom."[7]
—Martin Luther King Jr., March 25, 1965

On March 21, 1965, King led civil rights demonstrators across the Edmund Pettus bridge on a Selma to Montgomery march.

In 1964, King was awarded the Nobel Peace Prize medal.

BLACK POWER

*K*ing was awarded the 1964 Nobel Peace Prize and won worldwide admiration for his leadership of a peaceful resistance. In the ten years since the Montgomery bus boycott, the nonviolent civil rights movement had taken great strides forward. The most dramatic changes occurred in the Jim Crow South. Schools, businesses, and transportation all over the South had been integrated. Thousands of African Americans had registered to vote for the first time in their lives.

Black Power

In a 1966 speech, Stokely Carmichael stated:

"We been saying freedom for six years, and we ain't got nothin'. What we gonna start saying now is Black Power!"[1]

Blacks in areas outside the South felt the civil rights movement had done nothing for them. Because of housing discrimination, urban blacks found themselves confined to overcrowded ghettos run by slumlords. Unemployment and poverty were high, and incidents of police brutality caused a simmering anger. Weeks after the president signed the Voting Rights Act on August 6, 1965, anger erupted in the most violent riots the nation had ever seen.

WATTS RIOTS

On August 11, 1965, a police officer arrested a 21-year-old black man, Marquette Frye, for drunk driving in Watts, a poor black neighborhood in Los Angeles, California. This led to an argument that attracted onlookers. People began to throw rocks and bottles. As the angry mob grew, white-owned businesses were vandalized, looted, and burned.

Six days later, the riot subsided and 34 people were dead, more than 1,000 were injured, and more than 3,000 had been arrested. Most of the neighborhood businesses and some houses were destroyed.

Civil rights leaders condemned the rioting. As Lewis, leader of SNCC and later a congressman from Georgia, noted:

> *Rioting is not a movement. It is not an act of civil disobedience. . . . It's simply an explosion of emotion. That's all. There is nothing constructive about it. It is only destructive.*[2]

As senseless as the violence seemed, it was the expression of a very real sense of powerlessness and despair in the black community. "People keep calling it a riot, but we call it a revolt because it had a legitimate purpose. It was a response to police brutality and social exploitation of a community and of a people," explained Tommy Jacquette, one of the rioters. Then he continued,

> *We did not own this community. We did not own the businesses in this community. We did not own the majority of the housing in this community. Some people want to know if I think it was really worth it. I think any time people stand up for their rights, it's worth it.*[3]

*Black Muslim leader Malcolm X
held up a newspaper during a rally on August 6, 1963.*

THE CHANGING MOVEMENT

The rioting in US cities was just one indication that the civil rights movement was changing. A movement based on nonviolent resistance became increasingly more aggressive. Young people had grown impatient with the slow pace of change and were ready to demand their rights.

New leaders, such as Malcolm X, emerged in the late 1950s and gave expression to this idea. Malcolm was a charismatic activist and rose to fame as a member of the Nation of Islam. The goal of the organization was not integration with white society but a complete separation and establishment of an independent black nation. Malcolm was critical of King and other mainstream civil rights leaders. He believed they compromised too much with white oppressors. In a speech in late 1963, Malcolm dismissed the idea of nonviolent resistance as ineffective:

> You don't have a peaceful revolution. You don't have a turn-the-other-cheek revolution. There's no such thing. . . . Revolution is bloody, revolution is hostile. . . . And you [say], "I'm going to love these folks no matter how much they hate me." No, you need a revolution.[4]

Malcolm broke with the Nation of Islam in 1964 and moderated his views somewhat. He had visited Mecca, a Muslim holy site in Saudi Arabia where blacks and whites intermingled peacefully with mutual respect. Malcolm saw the possibility that blacks and whites could coexist. Still, he emphasized that nonviolence in the face of violence was not a workable solution. He urged blacks to arm themselves in self-defense. Some black groups were doing just that.

Black Militants

In 1965, after the march in Selma, SNCC leaders continued the fight for voting rights. A new project, similar to Mississippi Freedom Summer, was initiated in Lowndes County, Alabama. The KKK was so strong in the county that only one black person out of 12,000 had dared register to vote. As expected, the white racists continued to use violence to stop the project.

In August, a white minister working with SNCC was shot and killed. The murder pushed the group

Malcolm Little

Malcolm Little was born in 1925. When he was a baby, the KKK burned down his family's home in Omaha, Nebraska. In 1929, white supremacists killed his father. Malcolm was then raised in foster homes. At 20, he was sentenced to prison for burglary. While in prison, he joined the Nation of Islam—a black nationalist group led by Elijah Muhammad. He also became an avid reader. He later wrote, "Months passed without my even thinking about being imprisoned. In fact, up to then, I had never been so truly free in my life."[6]

Upon release from prison, he became a minister for the Nation of Islam. Rejecting his original surname, given to his ancestors by slave owners, he adopted the letter *X* as his name. An electrifying speaker, Malcolm became a leader for black rights. The media portrayed him as a teacher of hate because he advocated separation from white society. But Malcolm rejected this label, saying, "I'm *not* a racist. I'm not condemning whites for being whites, but for their deeds. I condemn what whites collectively have done to our people."[7] He broke with the Nation of Islam in 1964. In 1965, he was assassinated by Black Muslim rivals. His messages of black pride and independence still resonate among young people today.

to make two important decisions. SNCC leader
Stokely Carmichael recalled,

> *The project staff took the strong position . . . to allow whites*
> *in would be tantamount to inviting their deaths. That became*
> *our policy. And we armed ourselves.* [8]

In Alabama, SNCC had become an all-black
organization with guns to defend themselves. Other
black groups also adopted a more
militant stance. The best known was
the Black Panther Party for Self-
Defense. The group was founded
in Oakland, California, in October
1966, by Huey Newton and Bobby
Seale. Inspired by Malcolm, they
believed in freedom by any means,
including violence. The Black
Panthers wore military-style berets
and black leather jackets. Armed with
shotguns, they patrolled the streets
in Oakland to protest police brutality
and organized programs to help
the poor. Their emblem of a black
panther became known as a symbol of
the new Black Power movement.

Black Power

The Black Power
movement was not just
about militancy and the
use of violence to achieve
its goals. It was about racial
pride and self-esteem at a
time when blacks were
not treated equally. They
were encouraged to cre-
ate or become part of
black political parties and
acknowledge their cul-
tural history. By doing so,
they would become more
powerful in their goal
of social and economic
progress and power.

TOWARD THE PROMISED LAND

By 1967, violent riots such as the one in Watts broke out in dozens of cities including Newark, New Jersey; Detroit, Michigan; and Cleveland, Ohio. Opposition to the war in Vietnam was one reason for anger in the ghettos. At the time of the Vietnam War, between 1961 and 1966, African Americans comprised approximately 13 percent of the US population and approximately 10 percent of the US soldiers in Vietnam. In 1965, nearly 25 percent of those who died in Vietnam were African American. Anger increased as money to help the poor people in US cities was cut back to fund an unpopular war.

King had long spoken out against the war in Vietnam. He launched the Poor People's Campaign in December 1967. The goal of the campaign was to direct the government's attention and funding away from the war in Asia and toward helping poor people at home in the United States.

Black Panthers Take a Stand

In May 1967, the Black Panthers caused a sensation when they marched into the California statehouse in Sacramento armed with loaded shotguns. On the floor of the state assembly, Seale delivered a speech against gun control, which the Black Panthers believed was aimed at weakening the power of blacks to defend themselves. The gun control bill passed, but the Black Panthers felt they had made their point. "We set the example," founder Newton explained. "We made black people aware that they had the right to carry guns."[9]

In April 1968, King traveled to Memphis, Tennessee, to speak at a rally for black sanitation workers who had gone on strike. He called on black people to reunite and continue fighting for justice, with or without his leadership:

> *We've got some difficult days ahead. But it doesn't matter with me now. Because I've been to the mountaintop. . . . And I've seen the promised land. I may not get there with you. But I want you to know tonight, that we, as a people, will get to the promised land.*[10]

The next morning, April 4, 1968, King was killed. James Earl Ray, a white man, shot King on the balcony of his motel in Memphis. Rioting broke out once more as the nation mourned the death of the great leader.

With King's death, the civil rights movement lost its focus and momentum. The main drive of the movement came to a halt. However, activists from all over the United States continued to push for positive change. After 13 tumultuous years, African Americans had not reached the promised land. But along with King, they had glimpsed it and held out hope of reaching it one day. ⌐

King's widow, Coretta Scott King, attended a memorial service for her husband.

*In an interview in 2006, Senator Obama
considered the idea of running for president.*

CIVIL RIGHTS TODAY

Great strides have been made since King
spoke of his dream in 1963 at the March
on Washington. It is difficult to fully imagine what
it was like to live in the segregated society of the
1960s. Until the 1964 elections, only five members

of the US Congress were African Americans. Since African Americans gained their right to vote, many have become prominent politicians. As of the 2010 elections, 42 members of Congress are African Americans, compared with only six in 1968. In 2008, US Senator Barack Obama was elected as the nation's first African-American president.

Still, the struggle continues. African Americans, women, Latinos, Native Americans, Asian Americans, homosexuals, and people with disabilities are working for their civil rights. Muslim Americans have faced discrimination as people mistakenly label them as terrorists. Although many laws have changed to protect civil rights for all citizens, the reality is that discrimination and inequality still exist in our society.

UNEQUAL STANDARD OF LIVING AND EDUCATION

Today, African Americans represent some of the wealthiest people in our nation. These include American Express CEO Kenneth Chenault, television icon Oprah Winfrey, and sports stars such as Shaquille O'Neal and Kobe Bryant. Overall, however, blacks and other minorities are far more likely than whites to suffer from poverty and unemployment. Government statistics for 2010 indicate 24.7 percent of African Americans—nearly one out of four—live in poverty as do 23.2 percent of Latinos. In contrast, only 8.6 percent of whites live in poverty. By the end of 2009, approximately 25 percent of blacks and Latinos were either unemployed or underemployed— twice the number for whites. Black males are six times more likely than whites to be in prison.

Inequality in education contributes to the social and economic gap between minorities

Rights for All

Today, gay, lesbian, bisexual, and transgender (GLBT) people strive for acceptance in US society. Like other minorities, they face prejudice and discrimination. Until recently, gays and lesbians were banned from serving openly in the US military by a 1993 law known as "Don't ask, don't tell." The law was repealed in December 2010.

Currently, there is controversy regarding whether gay and lesbian couples should have the right to marry and be entitled to the same legal advantages, such as spousal health insurance, as married couples. Gay advocates claim marriage is a civil right guaranteed by the Fourteenth Amendment. Opponents argue the definition of marriage is a union between a man and a woman. As of 2011, only six states and Washington DC allowed same-sex marriages. Coretta Scott King worked for gay rights during her lifetime. In 1998, she said,

I still hear people say that I should not be talking about the rights of lesbian and gay people and I should stick to the issue of racial justice . . . But I hasten to remind them that Martin Luther King, Jr., said, "Injustice anywhere is a threat to justice everywhere" . . . I appeal to everyone . . . to make room at the table of brotherhood and sisterhood for lesbian and gay people.[1]

and whites. Segregation in public schools has been illegal since 1954. But the reality is that some schools across the United States remain segregated by race. A 2010 report by the Children's Defense Fund stated that 73 percent of black students and 78 percent of Hispanic or Latino students attend predominantly minority schools. Minority-dominated schools are generally in poorer neighborhoods. These schools often receive fewer funds from the government and offer a lower standard of education.

Affirmative Action

Affirmative action programs seek to correct past discrimination by providing greater opportunities for African Americans and other minorities in schools and the workplace. Some people argue affirmative action has led to reverse discrimination as schools and employers feel pressure to select a certain percentage of minorities in jobs, regardless of who is most qualified.

"I think we're at a crossroads for opportunity," stated Alan Jenkins, director and cofounder of the Opportunity Agenda, an organization that seeks to improve opportunities in America. He added,

> There are some areas where we've made great progress. For example, African American women have made the most progress of any group in college attendance—a remarkable success story. But in many other areas America is in real trouble. Great inequality and discrimination still exist in our school systems, our criminal justice system, and other aspects of our lives. [2]

Police Brutality and Racial Profiling

In 1991, Rodney King, an African-American, was brutally beaten by police in Los Angeles. After leading the police on a high-speed chase, according to police, he resisted arrest. The beating was captured on videotape by a bystander and widely shown in the media, causing outrage in the African-American community. The officers were put on trial and found not guilty of any crime. Hours after the verdict, a riot broke out in Los Angeles on April 29, 1992. The riot lasted six days and caused approximately $1 billion in property damage. Fifty-three people were killed and thousands were injured.

The 1992 riots in Los Angeles and the Watts riots of 1965 were sparked by African-American rage over what they felt was unequal treatment by law enforcement. Today, racial profiling remains an issue. Racial profiling is the targeting of certain racial or ethnic groups by law enforcement and other types of security. It is illegal and unconstitutional. The US

Discrimination

In December 2001, three months after the attacks of September 11, Assem Bayaa, an American citizen of Arab descent, boarded a United Airlines flight from Los Angeles to New York. He had successfully cleared all the security checks at the airport, but once on the plane, he was asked to leave because his presence made the other passengers nervous. Bayaa sued the airlines for discrimination. In 2005, the case was settled out of court.

Protestors demonstrated at police headquarters in Washington DC over the verdict in the Rodney King trial.

Constitution guarantees every person, regardless of race, the right to equal protection.

Racial profiling not only affects African Americans. People of Middle Eastern appearance or with Arabic-sounding names are more likely to be searched in airports. Following the September 11, 2001, terrorist attacks, a report by the Lawyers' Committee on Human Rights charged that the FBI had detained 1,200 Arabs and other Muslims for interrogation, none of which led to an arrest. Most detainees had no access to lawyers, which is a violation of a person's civil rights. In 2010, the American Civil Liberties Union (ACLU) challenged a new law in Arizona. The law required police to check the immigration status of people on routine traffic stops if they appeared to be illegally in the United States. The ACLU argued that the law amounted to racial profiling against Latinos.

A Supreme Court Ruling

In 2009, a US Supreme Court decision ruled that an attempt to eliminate potential discrimination in hiring a certain group of employees can be interpreted as discrimination against another group of employees.

The court's decision was made regarding firefighters in New Haven, Connecticut. By disregarding the results of a promotions test on which few minorities scored well, city officials violated the rights of the white firefighters who did score well.

IMPROVING OPPORTUNITIES

The 13 years from 1955 to 1968 marked the greatest period of social change to occur in US history. The progress was hard won and must be protected. Still, young people of all races, religions, and ethnic backgrounds—male or female, gay or straight—cannot take freedom for granted. The movement for civil rights is ongoing to secure equal treatment for all. The United States can be the land of freedom and opportunity only if every American is committed to making that promise true for everyone.

On April 25, 1993, people marched in the US capital for gay and lesbian rights and for an end to the US military's ban on gays in the armed services.

TIMELINE

1866	1870	1896
The Civil Rights Act guaranteed former slaves equality before the law.	The Fifteenth Amendment gives black males the right to vote.	In *Plessy v. Ferguson*, the Supreme Court rules racial segregation is legal, leading to the separate but equal policy.

1955	1956	1957
In December, Rosa Parks is arrested for refusing to give up her seat on a public bus to a white man.	The Supreme Court declares segregation of public buses illegal.	In January, the Southern Christian Leadership Conference is established. King is its first president.

1909

The NAACP is founded to combat racism in the court system.

1941

President Franklin D. Roosevelt signs an executive order banning discrimination in the government and defense industry.

1954

In *Brown v. Board of Education*, the Supreme Court rules segregation of public schools is illegal.

1957

In September, federal troops are called in to protect Little Rock Central High School students and enforce integration.

1960

On February 1, black students hold a sit-in at a whites-only lunch counter in North Carolina.

1961

Freedom Riders protest illegal bus segregation.

TIMELINE

1963

King is jailed
in Birmingham,
Alabama, on April 12.

1963

On June 11,
civil rights activist
Medgar Evers
is murdered
in Mississippi.

1963

On August 28,
at the March on
Washington, King
gives his "I Have a
Dream" speech.

1965

In August,
race riots take place
in Watts, a black
neighborhood of Los
Angeles, California.

1966

The Black Panthers
organization is
founded by Huey
Newton and Bobby
Seale in October.

1964

On July 2, President Lyndon B. Johnson signs the Civil Rights Act of 1964 into law.

1965

On March 7, police attack marchers in Selma, Alabama.

1965

President Johnson signs the Voting Rights Act into law on August 6.

1968

King is assassinated on April 4 in Memphis, Tennessee.

2008

The United States elects Barack Obama as its first African-American president.

Essential Facts

Date of Event

1955–1968

Place of Event

United States

Key Players

❖ Ralph Abernathy, minister in Montgomery, Alabama

❖ Stokely Carmichael, SNCC leader

❖ Orval Faubus, governor of Arkansas

❖ Fannie Lou Hamer, MFDP delegate

❖ Lyndon B. Johnson, US president (1963–1969)

❖ John F. Kennedy, US president (1961–1963)

❖ Martin Luther King Jr., minister in Montgomery, Alabama, and civil rights leader

❖ John Lewis, Freedom Rider and civil rights organizer

❖ Thurgood Marshall, US Supreme Court justice

❖ E. D. Nixon, civil rights leader in Montgomery, Alabama

❖ Rosa Parks, arrested for refusing to give up her seat on a bus to a white man

❖ George Wallace, governor of Alabama

❖ Malcolm X, Nation of Islam member

Highlights of Event

❖ In December 1955, Parks was arrested for refusing to give up her seat to a white man on a city bus in Montgomery, Alabama. The arrest led to a 381-day bus boycott and ultimately the desegregation of buses in Montgomery.

❖ In September 1957, Governor Faubus prevented nine black students from integrating Little Rock Central High School in Arkansas. Federal troops were called in to protect the students and enforce integration.

❖ In February 1960, four college students staged a sit-in at a whites-only lunch counter in Greensboro, North Carolina. The sit-in movement spread, leading to desegregation of restaurants and many other facilities throughout the South.

❖ In 1961, student volunteers known as Freedom Riders rode buses from Washington DC to New Orleans to protest illegal bus segregation.

❖ The March on Washington occurred on August 28, 1963. Nearly 250,000 people heard King give his "I Have a Dream" speech.

❖ On July 2, the Civil Rights Act of 1964 was signed into law by President Johnson.

❖ The Voting Rights Act was signed into law on August 6, 1965, by President Johnson.

Quote

"I have a dream that one day this nation will rise up and live out the true meaning of its creed: 'We hold these truths to be self-evident: that all men are created equal.' . . . I have a dream that my four little children will one day live in a nation where they will not be judged by the color of their skin but by the content of their character. . . . I have a dream today."—*Martin Luther King Jr.*

Glossary

abolish
To end or do away with.

boycott
To refuse to buy or use a service as a form of protest.

civil rights
The rights of a citizen.

commissioner
A government authority.

confrontation
A conflict of ideas or forces.

constitution
The body of laws that governs a nation or state.

constitutional amendment
A change to a constitution.

decree
A command or judicial order.

discrimination
Unequal or unfair treatment of people because of a difference such as sex or race.

emancipation
The act of setting someone free.

harass
To persistently annoy or attack another person.

integration
Mixing together, it is the opposite of segregation.

intervene
To interfere, usually by force or threat of force, in order to prevent an action.

Jim Crow laws
  Laws in the South that kept blacks separated from whites.

latitude
  A distance north or south of the equator that is measured in degrees.

lynching
  The murder of a person by a lawless mob, usually by hanging.

oppression
  The act of keeping a person or group of people down by force.

proclamation
  An official and formal order or decree.

racism
  The belief that one race is superior to other races.

segregation
  The act or policy of separating people based on race, sex, religious belief, or other characteristics.

sit-in
  A form of nonviolence in which participants occupy an area and refuse to leave.

suffrage
  The right to vote.

unconstitutional
  Going against the constitution or the main body of laws that govern a nation or state.

ADDITIONAL RESOURCES

SELECTED BIBLIOGRAPHY

Carson, Clayborne, and David J. Garrow. *The Eyes on the Prize Civil Rights Reader.* New York: Penguin, 1991. Print.

King, Coretta Scott. *My Life with Martin Luther King, Jr.* 1969. New York: Holt, 1993. Print.

Rubel, David. *The Coming Free: The Struggle for African-American Equality.* New York: DK, 2005. Print.

Williams, Juan. *Eyes on the Prize: America's Civil Rights Years, 1954–1965.* 1987. New York: Penguin, 2002. Print.

FURTHER READINGS

Parks, Rosa, with Jim Haskins. *Rosa Parks: My Story.* New York: Puffin, 1992. Print.

Partridge, Elizabeth. *Marching for Freedom.* New York: Viking, 2009. Print.

X, Malcolm, and Alex Haley. *The Autobiography of Malcolm X.* New York: Ballantine, 1964. Print.

Web Links

To learn more about the civil rights movement, visit ABDO Publishing Company online at **www.abdopublishing.com**. Web sites about the civil rights movement are featured on our Book Links page. These links are routinely monitored and updated to provide the most current information available.

Places to Visit

Birmingham Civil Rights Institute

520 Sixteenth Street North, Birmingham, AL 35203
205-328-9696
http://www.bcri.org
The Birmingham Civil Rights Institute is a museum and research center created in 1992 to educate the public about the civil rights struggle of the 1950s and 1960s.

Martin Luther King Jr. National Historic Site

450 Auburn Avenue Northeast, Atlanta, GA 30312
404-331-6922
http://www.nps.gov/nr/travel/atlanta/kin.htm
This historic site is a national park in downtown Atlanta. It was created to honor the memory of Martin Luther King Jr. and educate people about his work. Visitors can see King's birth home and his final resting place. The King Center, established in 1968 by Coretta Scott King, is also on the park's grounds.

National Civil Rights Museum

450 Mulberry Street, Memphis, TN 38103
901-521-9699
http://www.civilrightsmuseum.org
The museum is located in the former Lorraine Motel where Martin Luther King Jr. was assassinated in 1968. Key episodes of the civil rights movement are presented in interactive exhibits.

Source Notes

Chapter 1. "I Have a Dream"

1. "Patience is a Dirty and Nasty Word." *Eyes on the Prize: America's Civil Rights Movement 1954-1985*. PBS Online/WGBH, 2006. Web. 23 Feb. 2011.

2. Everett M. Dirksen. "Congress and the Civil Rights Act of 1964." N.p.,n.d. Web. 18 Apr. 2011.

3. Juan Williams. *Eyes on the Prize: America's Civil Rights Years, 1954–1965*. 1987. New York: Penguin, 2002. Print. 203–205.

4. Ibid.

5. Ibid.

Chapter 2. From Slavery to Segregation

1. "The Declaration of Independence." *USHistory.org*. Independence Hall Association, 2011. Web. 9 Feb. 2011.

2. Martin Luther King Jr. National Historic Site Interpretive Staff. "Examples of Jim Crow Laws" *Race, Racism and the Law*. Vernellia R. Randall, 2001. Web. 9 Feb. 2011.

3. David Rubel. *The Coming Free: The Struggle for African–American Equality*. New York: DK, 2005. Print. 17.

4. Sarah Hopkins Bradford. *Harriet, the Moses of Her People*. 1886. New York: Citadel, 2000. Print. 29.

Chapter 3. The Montgomery Bus Boycott

1. Rosa Parks and Jim Haskins. *Rosa Parks: My Story*. New York: Puffin, 1992. Print. 115.

2. Ibid. 116.

3. Ibid.

4. E. D. Nixon. Interview. "Awakenings (1954–1956)." *Eyes on the Prize: America's Civil Rights Years, 1954–1985*. PBS Online/WGBH, 2006. Web. 26 Jan. 2011. Transcript.

5. Juan Williams. *Eyes on the Prize: America's Civil Rights Years, 1954–1965*. 1987. New York: Penguin, 2002. Print. 68.

6. Coretta Scott King. *My Life with Martin Luther King Jr.* 1969. New York: Holt, 1993. Print. 108.

7. Ibid.

8. Martin Luther King Jr. *Strength to Love.* 1963. Minneapolis, MN: Augsburg, 2010. Print. 47.

Chapter 4. Crisis in Little Rock

1. Daisy Bates. *The Long Shadow of Little Rock.* 1962. Fayetteville: U of Arkansas P, 1986. Print. 75.

2. "Terrence Roberts." *America.gov.* US Department of State Bureau of International Information Programs, 30 Aug. 2007. Web. 26 Jan. 2011.

3. Daisy Bates. *The Long Shadow of Little Rock.* 1962. Fayetteville: U of Arkansas P, 1986. Print. 75.

4. Juan Williams. *Eyes on the Prize: America's Civil Rights Years, 1954–1965.* 1987. New York: Penguin, 2002. Print. 109.

5. Daisy Bates. *The Long Shadow of Little Rock.* 1962. Fayetteville: U of Arkansas P, 1986. Print. 61.

6. Juan Williams. *Eyes on the Prize: America's Civil Rights Years, 1954–1965.* 1987. New York: Penguin, 2002. Print. 113.

7. Ernest Green. Northfield Mount Hermon School, Mount Hermon, MA. 19 Jan. 2011. NMSchool.org. 26 Jan. 2011. Speech.

Chapter 5. Sit-Ins and Freedom Rides

1. "Interview with Franklin McCain." *The Eyes on the Prize Civil Rights Reader.* Ed. Clayborne Carson, et al. New York: Penguin, 1991. Print. 115.

2. Juan Williams. *Eyes on the Prize: America's Civil Rights Years, 1954–1965.* 1987. New York: Penguin, 2002. Print. 131.

3. "Interview with Franklin McCain." *The Eyes on the Prize Civil Rights Reader.* Ed. Clayborne Carson, et al. New York: Penguin, 1991. Print. 115.

4. Ibid.

5. Juan Williams. *Eyes on the Prize: America's Civil Rights Years, 1954–1965.* 1987. New York: Penguin, 2002. Print. 135.

6. David Rubel. *The Coming Free: The Struggle for African-American Equality.* New York: DK, 2005. Print. 146.

SOURCE NOTES CONTINUED

7. Juan Williams. *Eyes on the Prize: America's Civil Rights Years, 1954–1965.* 1987. New York: Penguin, 2002. Print. 149–151.

8. Ibid. 158.

9. Ibid. 155.

Chapter 6. The Birmingham Campaign

1. Marshall Frady. *Martin Luther King Jr: A Life.* New York: Penguin, 2002. Print 98.

2. Ibid.

3. Juan Williams. *Eyes on the Prize: America's Civil Rights Years, 1954–1965.* 1987. New York: Penguin, 2002. Print. 187.

4. Ibid. 188–189.

5. Irma McClaurin and Virginia Schomp. *The Civil Rights Movement.* New York: Benchmark, 2008. Print. 49.

6. Juan Williams. *Eyes on the Prize: America's Civil Rights Years, 1954–1965.* 1987. New York: Penguin, 2002. Print. 188.

Chapter 7. The Right to Vote

1. "The Case for Lyndon B. Johnson." *Ebony.* Chicago: Johnson, Nov. 1964. Print. 70.

2. David Rubel. *The Coming Free: The Struggle for African-American Equality.* New York: DK, 2005. Print. 236–237.

3. Ibid. 241.

4. Fannie Lou Hamer. "To Praise Our Bridges." *The Eyes on the Prize Civil Rights Reader.* Ed. Clayborne Carson, et al. New York: Penguin, 1991. Print. 177.

5. Elizabeth Partridge. *Marching for Freedom.* New York: Viking, 2009. Print. 30.

6. Irma McClaurin and Virginia Schomp. *The Civil Rights Movement.* New York: Benchmark, 2008. Print. 65.

7. Elizabeth Partridge. *Marching for Freedom.* New York: Viking, 2009. Print. 53.

Chapter 8. Black Power

1. David Rubel. *The Coming Free: The Struggle for African-American Equality*. New York: DK, 2005. Print. 278.

2. Milton Meltzer. *There Comes a Time: The Struggle for Civil Rights*. New York: Random, 2001. Print. 151.

3. Valerie Reitman and Mitchell Landsberg. "Watts Riots: 40 Years Later." *Los Angeles Times*. www.latimes.com/about, 11 Aug. 2005. Web. 26 Jan. 2011.

4. Malcolm X. "Message to the Grass Roots." *The Eyes on the Prize Civil Rights Reader*. Ed. Clayborne Carson, et al. New York: Penguin, 1991. Print. 253.

5. Malcolm X. *By Any Means Necessary: Speeches*. Ed. George Breitman. New York: Pathfinder, 1992. Print. 9.

6. Malcolm X and Alex Haley. *The Autobiography of Malcolm X*. New York: Ballantine, 1964. Print. 199.

7. Ibid. 475.

8. David Rubel. *The Coming Free: The Struggle for African-American Equality*. New York: DK, 2005. Print. 269.

9. Ibid. 281.

10. Martin Luther King Jr. "To the Mountaintop." Mason Temple, Memphis. 3 Apr. 1968. AmericanRhetoric.com. Web. 26 Jan. 2011. Speech.

Chapter 9. Civil Rights Today

1. Corretta Scott King. Speech for 25th anniversary luncheon for Lambda Defense and Education Fund. soulforce.com. Web. 31 Mar. 1998.

2. Alan Jenkins. Interview by Maria Daniels. WGBH, Boston. July 2006. PBS Online/WGBH. Web. 26 Jan. 2011.

INDEX

ABOUT THE AUTHOR

Jennifer Joline Anderson has been writing since she was a teenager, when she won a contest and had her first short story published in *Seventeen* magazine. She lives in Minneapolis, Minnesota, where she writes and edits educational books and other nonfiction for young people.

PHOTO CREDITS

Robert W. Kelley/Time & Life Pictures/Getty Images, cover, 3; AP Images, 6, 8, 13, 26, 41, 54, 61, 67, 68, 81, 96 (bottom), 98 (top), 99 (top left); Kean Collection/Getty Images, 14; Library of Congress, 19, 96 (top); Hulton Archive/Getty Images, 25; Don Cravens/Time & Life Pictures/Getty Images, 30; New York Times Co./Getty Images, 35; Red Line Editorial, 36, 97 (top); MPI/Getty Images, 45; Donald Uhrbrock/Time & Life Pictures/Getty Images, 46, 97 (bottom); Truman Moore/Time & Life Pictures/Getty Images, 51; Paul Schutzer/Time & Life Pictures/Getty Images, 57; Horace Cort/AP Images, 58; Bill Hudson/AP Images, 64; AFP/Getty Images, 77, 78, 99 (top right); Jim Bourdier/AP Images, 87, 99 (bottom); Pablo Martinez Monsivais/AP Images, 88; Paul J. Richards/AFP/Getty Images, 93; Mark Wilson/AP Images, 95